BE NICE TO YOUR MUM
MOTHERF*CKERS

Jenny Wynter

COPYRIGHT © 2024 JENNY WYNTER.
ALL RIGHTS RESERVED.
NO PART OF THIS BOOK MAY BE REPRODUCED OR TRANSMITTED IN ANY FORM OR BY ANY MEANS, ELECTRONIC OR MECHANICAL, INCLUDING PHOTOCOPYING, RECORDING, OR BY ANY INFORMATION STORAGE AND RETRIEVAL SYSTEM, WITHOUT WRITTEN PERMISSION FROM THE AUTHOR.

ANY RESEMBLANCE TO ACTUAL PERSONS, LIVING OR DEAD, OR ACTUAL EVENTS IS PURELY COINCIDENTAL.

IF YOU BELIEVE THAT YOU HAVE BEEN REPRESENTED IN THIS BOOK, CALL YOUR MUM. SOON.

FOR INFORMATION WWW.JENNYWYNTER.COM

PRINTED IN AUSTRALIA
2 4 6 8 10 9 7 5 3 1

THIS BOOK IS DEDICATED TO
ALL THE EXHAUSTED WOMEN
WHO DESERVE BETTER.

AND FOR JAS AND HELEN.
I LOVE YOU.

BE NICE TO YOUR MUM, MOTHERF*CKERS

'COS WHETHER YOU KNOW IT OR NOT

SHE'S THERE EVEN WHEN YOU'RE A SHIT SHOW

EVEN WHEN YOU'RE THE WORLD'S BIGGEST SNOT.

BE NICE TO YOUR MUM, MOTHERF*CKERS

SHE'S DONE MORE FOR YOU THAN YOU CAN KNOW

FROM THE DAY YOU WERE CUTE 'TIL YOU TURNED TO A BRUTE

SHE STAYED WHEN SHE WANTED TO GO.

BE NICE TO YOUR MUM, MOTHERF*CKERS

IT'S REALLY NOT ASKING THAT MUCH

SHE SHOWED UP FOR YOU SICK, SAD OR STRESSED OUT

EVEN THOUGH YOU FULL RUINED HER CROTCH.

BE NICE TO YOUR MUM, MOTHERF*CKERS

SHE'S NOT PERFECT BUT NEITHER ARE YOU

YET BEYOND UNDERSTANDING, THAT WOMAN'S STILL STANDING

DESPITE ALL THE SHIT THAT YOU THREW.

YOU MAY NOT KNOW NOW, MOTHERF*CKERS

BUT EVENTUALLY THAT DAY WILL COME

YOU'LL BE OLDER AND WISER, SO EVEN IF YOU DESPISE HER

FOR F*CK'S SAKE

BE NICE TO YOUR MUM

www.ingramcontent.com/pod-product-compliance
Lightning Source LLC
Chambersburg PA
CBHW041525070526
44585CB00002B/90